My House
Is
Black Feathers

poems by

Sally Doyle

Finishing Line Press
Georgetown, Kentucky

My House
Is
Black Feathers

Copyright © 2019 by Sally Doyle
ISBN 978-1-64662-098-2 First Edition
All rights reserved under International and Pan-American Copyright Conventions. No part of this book may be reproduced in any manner whatsoever without written permission from the publisher, except in the case of brief quotations embodied in critical articles and reviews.

ACKNOWLEDGMENTS

For Tim who is never surprised when he opens the door to find Crow and I in deep conversation.

Publisher: Leah Maines
Editor: Christen Kincaid
Cover Art: Sally Doyle
Author Photo: Tim Doyle
Cover Design: Elizabeth Maines McCleavy

Printed in the USA on acid-free paper.
Order online: www.finishinglinepress.com
          also available on amazon.com

Author inquiries and mail orders:
Finishing Line Press
P. O. Box 1626
Georgetown, Kentucky 40324
U. S. A.

Table of Contents

Songs from Crow's Song 1

No One to Reach 2

What Crow Taught Me 3

It Happened Often 4

Ashes 5

Body Tricks 6

Instructions 7

Can't Laugh 8

Sinking Hole 9

Dancing Sticks 10

Pollen 11

Crow Diver 12

Startled 13

Black Cloud 14

Saint of Inconsolable Souls 15

Cranial Guitar Man 17

Practice 18

Grief 19

House of Knowing Yourself 20

My Book Is Girl 21

What Ghost? 22

Lullaby 23

Hunger's Shadow 24

Epilogue 25

*The poet lives in the midst of death
and seeks the mystery of life...*
　　　　Bob Kaufman

Songs from Crow's Song

I am not up for this.

So.

Just saying.

Said. Go on then.

*Crow visited my dream,
circled in the dream's interior
screeching.*

You must now make songs from his song.

*But those would be songs of punishment,
sounds of pain.*

Would you rather not sing at all?

I want to sing of beautiful things.

On the third day of the world,
that's what Crow wished too.

Why didn't you give Crow his wish?

Because Crow wouldn't be Crow
if he sang another way.

No One to Reach

There is no one to reach.
Owl high in the branches.
Here you are poking around on a mound of earth
with large sounds crawling over you.
Sky swarms with birds
and invisible footsteps.
Even if you throw pebbles into blue water,
Lake spirits will not answer—
not even if you swim all the way
down to the bottom.
But, now you know how to
pull your blanket through winter,
you know the sound of miles.

What Crow Taught Me

I crouch under a pine
wearing animal thoughts.
The squirrels are playing
games all over the place.
I know how to turn into a squirrel,
but don't want to today.
I don't feel like playing games or
cracking nuts open with my teeth.
There is something else going on,
an unknown sound creeping closer.

Long ago, as a baby, Crow showed up
when no one else was in the room.
I listened to him talk a lot,
but he wasn't saying
In God We Trust or anything like that.
No way. He explained to me how to
wake in a different body.
He taught me how to be animal again,
how to lay my ears on the ground
to hear who's coming.

It Happened Often

They were away not really caring
where I was or what I was doing.
 As a child, I knew when they didn't remember me.
This knowledge happened in my body,
in a place that could not speak.
It happened often,
and every time it did
Crow watched me carefully
with his cold, black eyes.

Ashes

The animals are laughing,
even though they are stuck in black ashes.
To begin with, who left their bones here?
Sometimes your whole life gets into a boat
and rows to the other shore without you.
How could you let this happen?
I lined up the bottles on the counter.
By morning, the wind had blown
the rest of the world away.

Body Tricks

Last night my feet became wind and took off.
They had always wanted to go running over treetops,
and probably thought this was their chance.
My heart was already out there floating in moonlight.
My mouth said it was thirsty and left too.
It hurt that my body parts wandered so far away at times.

*Hey, how about me? Didn't it even occur
to you that I might want to go out walking too?*
No one answered me so I laid waiting with my
creaking bones under a heavy blanket.
When the sun peeked over the horizon, I started crying.
What if these parts of myself don't come back?

I heard giggling under the covers
so I peeked under. Feet and Heart were laughing it up.
Mouth was laughing too. *We tricked you,* they teased.
We were here the whole night.

I didn't believe them, but in the light of day,
I didn't feel upset anymore. We all went walking
the woods together, and no one said a thing about the night before.
We strolled happily through the trees,
saying good morning to everyone we met
until Belly growled, and we went to find breakfast.

Instructions

I had received this instruction:
PAY THE PRICE.
Little pieces stuck down my throat.
Wind had other ideas:
HOWL UNTIL NOTHING IS LEFT.
Now my clothes are up in a tree
standing among the branches as
if I were still inside of them.
My name has broken free and
circles above with Crow.

Can't Laugh

One day I woke up, and couldn't laugh.
I knew it right away.
Laughter had left me to go somewhere else.
I had to go everywhere with a grumpy look on my face.
Many who saw me said, *"Oh, you have that look again."*

My friends and family tried to make me happy.
They missed my sunny laugh.
They got up to all sorts of antics to bring it back.
Wolf walked on his back paws.
Bear mimicked duck and quacked, (but his quack had a growl in it).
Raven put on Crow's mask, but no one really noticed.
My brother piled dead grass on his head
and ran around with his pants falling down.
None of these antics, however, got a *ha* out of me.

They gave up trying, and decided to hold a ceremony
to officially change my name *to Can't Laugh.*
They circled around me with their arms raised to the sky
announcing my new name to each direction.
And that's what did it—I started laughing!
Why this ceremony made me laugh, I don't know.
But, it did. I laughed so hard my new name,
Can't Laugh, fell off me. It wouldn't stick, and
that made me laugh harder.
That's the shortest time anyone had kept a name before.

Sinking Hole

Everyday I disappoint my
mother's ashes.
I disappoint the hours in the day
with my sad heart, and I disappoint each night
with fears and nightmares.
How can I find light with the noise of
shame strapped to my body?

All I can do is imitate the animals inside me—
take the antlers from the top of the
mountain and put them on my head.
Charge down the steep rocks with Moon on my back.

This most likely won't satisfy the others,
but I might surrender something I haven't before.
And it could be that Old Badger with his muddy face
might push all my disappointment into Sinking Hole.

Dancing Sticks

I was upset, so I went to the pond where turtles live.
As soon as I got there I could see
that the sticks were dancing again.
Why did the sticks have to flaunt their happiness?
It hurt that the sticks danced in the midst of all my troubles.
They danced with excitement and intensity.
Their inner light and freedom glowed from within.
I knew they would keep dancing
no matter what; even in the fierce storm
that was blowing in.
This made me so mad that I stomped
 on the sticks to make them stop.
But of course those sticks kept dancing
which left me with no choice, but to plop myself
down in the mud and enjoy the show!

Pollen

The pollen hadn't gotten hold of me for a long time.
All the bees were buzzing somewhere else.
They were so far away I couldn't hear them anymore.
Then one day I turned into a bee, and buzzed straight
over to the yellow, sun-opened rose in my garden.
I crawled inside to its center packed with pollen.
Dizzy, and with unspeakable joy,
I loaded my baskets with pollen
until they were full and spilling.
When I staggered out through the fragrant petals,
I had pollen in my hair and between my toes.
It was even on my lips.

Crow Driver

Crow sits on top of the Wells Fargo building
taking inventory:
heaps of broken furniture and torn clothes
pizza boxes dog shit
men and women with lost identities
worn shoes and stained mattresses
garbage mountains
rust working its way up fences
plastic bottles rolling in the gutter
newspapers sailing in the wind.
This territory belongs to him.
Cawing three times—
he is ready to dive.

Startled

Moonlight behind tall trees,
popping out to spook me.
I take off running,
afraid of looking back.
Falling leaves startle me.
So do bird cries.

What was that?
I stop.
My rigid body unable
to move breath in or out.
Maybe I'm not born yet.
Maybe I am already dead.

Black Cloud

I look out the window. Trouble!
Storm Cloud's dressed
in black feathers shouting thunder.

Then, this circumstance happened:
day after day I am going to die.
Ladder of broken rungs,
handprint on window glass, black feather.
I am the shape of what can't last.

Saint of Inconsolable Souls

Crow likes to put himself inside my mind
He dances on madness.
Lunatic language is sacred to him.
Crow is a black crackling nation of poets.
He is Bob Kaufman.
He is Buddha.
Then, he is a patient in a hospital
where everything has gone wrong.

He takes notes, documenting everything.
Tonight he observes my sad
collapse inward,
my fear and disequilibrium, and then wanders
to the part of my brain where I grew up—
the exact time and place in my head
where it continues—
the captured landscape,
the boiling sea, the animal
with its amputated leg,
me.

Crow takes it all in with his steel eyes—
my hair is full of burning thistles,
my heart shut behind one thousand doors.
He doesn't startle me.
He knows how to be close to the wounded,
conversing with their silence and pain.

Crow is the Saint of Inconsolable Souls:
Crow has been with many others before:
Crow of John Keats and Emily Bronte,
of Virginia Woolf and Franz Kafka,
of Herman Melville and Marina Tsvetaeva.

Crow of Samuel Taylor Coleridge and Federico Garcia Lorca,
of Gerard Manley Hopkins and Emily Dickinson.

Crow of Clarice Lispector and Walt Whitman,
of Paul Celan and Anonymous,
Crow of No One.

Crow is the saint of neurotics and the lonely,
of ruined bodies and nightmares,
of sobbing and broken glass,
of death and brilliance.
Crow is the saint of the unloved.

He can't keep the hurt away,
but I need his presence tonight,
his beautiful determination
to know all the dark that exists.

Cranial Guitar Man

Would you wear my eyes?
My body is a torn mattress,
Disheveled throbbing place
For the coming and goings
of loveless transients.
                    Bob Kaufman

This is what scares me.
It is scar.
Not water. Not art.
Not hope. Just terror.

Who put this war in my body?

Rooms collapse one by one.
My wrist drips.
I lay down under the icy moon with Cranial Guitar Man,
and watch the *glowing minnows swim from his mouth.*
I roll his eyes around in my skull.
I am a disheveled throbbing place too,
I will wear your eyes until I can't go out any more.
Then, who will wear my eyes?

Practice

I am the woman in the center of the circle
with Rattling Gourd singing over me.
Then, *whoosh*- thrown into space
one thousand miles per hour.

People poke their sticks
over the empty place I've left behind.
They don't want to imagine
where I've gone off to
or what I'm doing.
They turn toward home to cook dinner.

Old Woman and Crow
are the only ones waiting when I return.
They don't console me
or pull me free from spirits
who marked my face.
They understand it's only the beginning.
I must practice this way,
alone without anyone watching.

It will take time to learn
 how to let my bones and words evaporate,
so I become light enough
for Wind to carry me.

Grief

I go walking
with Grief—
straight down
where emptiness catches fire.

On and on,
I continue,
until I arrive at the door
where old woman sits
rocking tiny bones
of every blackbird
that has fallen
out of the sky.

House of Knowing Yourself

Where is the house of knowing yourself?
In the shrine a wall has broken off.
What's going on?

Don't let it be sorrow.

In every window Rumi saw
God's face.
Even in his sleep Rumi
kept his secret eye open
in case God came wandering by.

How did he do that?

Down by the river
Old Woman
is spinning with good fortune and love.
Birds fly up from her twirling skirt hem.
She is turning the waterwheel of her heart.
Every bone in her body is turning with her.
Her birth and death are turning with her.

That's how Old Woman does it.

My Book Is Girl

Who is heading East?
Nobody's there.
Pray for me.
Who is heading West?
Fire Spirit.
Pray for me. Pray for me.
It's past midnight,
I hear her coming, volcanic rocks
in the back of her truck.
Pray for me.

Early on, and frozen with fear,
I was sent into the darkness where Crow lives.
I had no choice. It wasn't up to me.
Crow kept moving things around me.
I couldn't see what he was moving, thumps
on the stairs, doors opening and closing.

That early time has followed me here.
I light the lamp, sweep ashes from the floor,
prop myself up at the table.
My book is absence. My book is scar.
My book is a tribute to the girl
who writes in the center of my life.

What Ghost?

The pond is flying towards me,
all bright and noisy.
My walking embedded in cliffs.
Split seconds of grassland
with longer moments of blue sky.
My breath, steep, rocky.

What ghost will use my breath after I'm gone?
What ghost will use my arms to glide
through the air or dive deep into the earth?
What ghost will ride
my nervous brown horse
into my everything
gone?

Lullaby

I lie down in the meadow.
Crow swoops down to land
on my chest   gently.

Crow likes riding up and down
on my breaths—
He says he feels like a surfer
resting on his board in the water.
He likes being lifted by air
and quietly put down again
in the almost dark of evening.

I'm so tired, I said, *from wanting to know everything.*
I feel the bitterness of the mountain in my throat.

Crow closes my eyes with his wings.
Hush, he says, *I will take care of you.*
I like the night when fish stars swim through sky,
and Moon tells indefatigable stories—
even after a bad day, Moon tells stories.

Hunger's Shadow

Crow flies into dense fog,
all boundaries gone.
Deep into absence he flies,
a scrap of blackness
whose cry
pierces this world
with hunger.

Epilogue

Tonight

down the long, straight gravel road
Crow and I stop the car and listen
to cornfields. Our listening
rustles (in the) warm breeze.
It lights (on) every ear like a candle.

Sally **Doyle** lives in San Francisco with her husband. She works as a poet in the schools.

She is currently a poet-in-residence at UCSF Benioff Children's Hospitals in San Francisco and Oakland California.

www.ingramcontent.com/pod-product-compliance
Lightning Source LLC
LaVergne TN
LVHW041516070426
835507LV00012B/1620